W9-ABM-238
3 0301 00034802 5

THE
TRADITION OF VIRGIL

LONDON: HUMPHREY MILFORD
OXFORD UNIVERSITY PRESS

THE TRADITION OF VIRGIL

Three Papers on the History and Influence of the Poet

BY

JUNIUS S. MORGAN
KENNETH McKENZIE
CHARLES G. OSGOOD

PRINCETON UNIVERSITY PRESS
MCMXXX

PRINTED AT THE PRINCETON UNIVERSITY PRESS, PRINCETON, NEW JERSEY, U.S.A.

PREFACE

N Virgil's birthday, the fifteenth of October, 1929, a company of the poet's friends in Princeton assembled to do him honor. The meeting was arranged by the Department of Classics and the presiding officer was John Grier Hibben, President of the University. The three addresses delivered on that occasion, though widely different in character, nevertheless had a certain unity because one and all dealt with the same general theme, the history and influence of the poet. Through the generosity of donors who have wished to remain anonymous these addresses are here published together as a contribution to the Bimillennial of Virgil's birth which is being commemorated this year throughout the world.

In a very real sense Virgil has lived through all the ages. To him has come in fullest measure that immortality for which the Roman poets often yearned—a life on the lips and in the hearts of men. It has been truly said of Cicero that in comparison with his after life his existence on this earth shrinks into nothingness. The remark is even more true of Virgil. From the date of his death, 19 B.C., at the comparatively early age of fifty-one, down through the centuries of the Roman Empire, the Middle Ages, and the Renaissance into our own time the tradition of him has been unbroken. For all who have been conscious of the classical heritage he has continued to be, as it were, a living personality. To this still living Virgil on the greatest of his anniversaries we offer the present volume as a modest birthday gift and with confidence in his future we make our own the good wishes which a friend of his sent on a like occasion to the great Messalla,

> at tu, Natalis multos celebrande per annos,
> candidior semper candidiorque veni.

Arthur Leslie Wheeler

Plate I

Mosaic Portrait of Virgil

THE HISTORY OF THE TEXT OF VIRGIL

IT IS my purpose to say a few words about the history of the text of Virgil's poems; but, first of all, I want to show you the portrait of the poet himself (Plate 1). This is the earliest authentic likeness of Virgil and, according to Gauckler,[1] dates about the end of the first century of our era. It is in mosaic and was unearthed at Soussa in Tunisia, in 1896, while the foundations for a new arsenal were being constructed. With its frame it measures about forty inches square.

As you see, Virgil is represented as seated, holding on his knees a roll of papyrus on which is written in cursive letters the following:

> "Musa mihi causas memora quo numine laeso,
> Quidve."

On his right stands Clio who is reading to him, and on his left Melpomene who is listening attentively. The poet has the expression of one inspired. As a work of art this mosaic is of very great interest, but, as a portrait of Virgil, its importance is even greater. Furthermore, it is the only one of its epoch in existence which, considering the esteem in which Virgil was held, is odd. As Gauckler says:[2] "What a strange thing that we should know the features of this popular poet, who had become a classic even before his death, only by the short and vague description given of him by Donatus and by some verses in the *Satires* of Horace! Yet his bust from the first century on adorned schools and public libraries. Alexander Severus went so far as to put the poet's statue in a chapel, and his fame,

[1] *Monuments et Memoires Piot*, IV (1897), 238.
[2] *ibid.*

having found favor with the fathers of the Church, preserved its brilliancy through the middle ages."

When I visited Tunis in 1910, this mosaic was in the Museum there and I presume still is. I refer anyone who is interested to Gauckler's article "Les Mosaïques Virgiliennes de Sousse" in *Monuments et Memoires* of the Fondation Piot, Volume IV, 1897, pages 233-44, and Plate xx.

Let us now turn to the consideration of the text of Virgil's poems and see how they have come down to us. In this connection, it is interesting to note that the amount of testimony both as to the number and importance of the manuscripts of Virgil is greater than in the case of any other author of pagan antiquity.[3]

It seems certain that Virgil himself wrote out his poems in their best form; at all events, Aulus Gellius, in the second century of our era, speaks about persons who had seen the original autograph manuscript of the *Georgics*.[4]

After Virgil's death in B.C. 19, his friends Varius and Tucca were entrusted with the publication of the *Æneid*. Publication would mean, of course, that scribes were given the autograph manuscript to copy and that these transcripts were copied in turn, a process which continued until the invention of printing.

The knowledge that we have of the text of Virgil's poems today is based, principally, on the following seven manuscripts:

(1) Codex Augusteus—designated by Ribbeck in his *Prolegomena ad Vergili Opera* by the letter "A"
(2) Schedae Vaticanae No. 3225—Ribbeck "F"
(3) Codex Mediceus—Ribbeck "M"
(4) Codex Romanus, Vaticanus No. 3867—Ribbeck "R"
(5) Codex Palatinus, Vaticanus No. 1631—Ribbeck "P"
(6) Schedae Sangallenses rescriptae—Ribbeck "G"
(7) Schedae Veronenses rescriptae—Ribbeck "V"

Not one of these manuscripts gives a complete text of Virgil and, as Professor Schanz remarks in his *Geschichte der römischen Littera-*

[3] Falconer Madan, *Books in Manuscript* (ed. 2, London, 1920), 79.
[4] *Noctes Atticae*, IX, 14.7; XIII, 21.4.

Plate II

Schedae Vaticanae, 3225: *Æneid* IV, 305–310

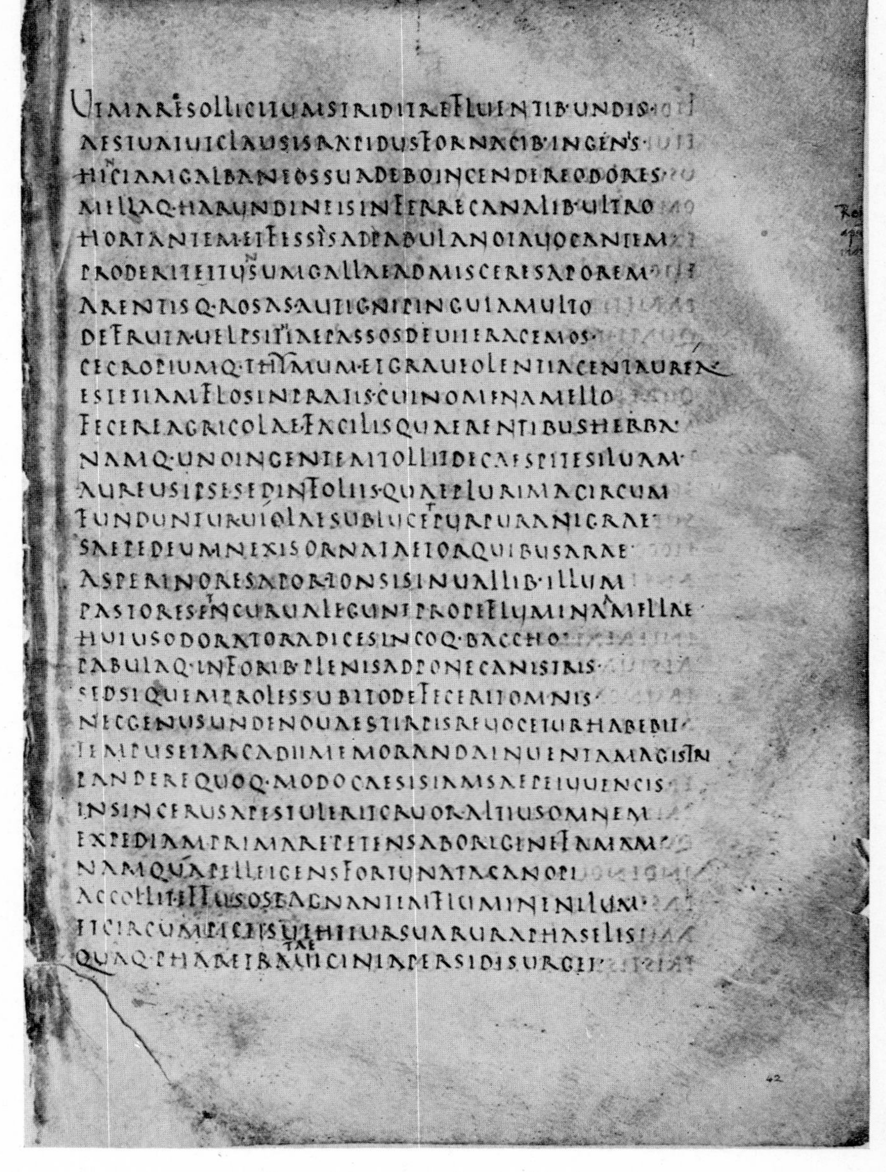

UTMARESOLLICITUMSTRIDITREFLUENTIBUNDIS
AESTUATUTCLAUSISRAPIDUSFORNACIBINGENS
HICIAMGALBANEOSSUADEBOINCENDEREODORES
MELLAQHARUNDINEISINFERRECANALIBULTRO
HORTANTEMETFESSASADPABULANOTAUOCANTEM
PRODERITETTUNSUMGALLAEADMISCERESAPOREM
ARENTISQROSASAUTIGNIPINGUIAMULTO
DEFRUTAUELPSITHIAPASSOSDEUITERACEMOS
CECROPIUMQTHYMUMETGRAUEOLENTIACENTAUREA
ESTETIAMFLOSINPRATISCUINOMENAMELLO
FECEREAGRICOLAEFACILISQUAERENTIBUSHERBA
NAMQUNOINGENTEMTOLLITDECAESPITESILUAM
AUREUSIPSESEDINFOLIISQUAEPLURIMACIRCUM
FUNDUNTURUIOLAESUBLUCETPURPURANIGRAE
SAEPEDEUMNEXISORNATAETORQUIBUSARAE
ASPERINORESAPORTONSISINUALLIBILLUM
PASTORESETCURUALEGUNTPROPEFLUMINAMELLAE
HUIUSODORATORADICESINCOQBACCHO
PABULAQINFORIBPLENISAPPONECANISTRIS
SEDSIQUEMPROLESSUBITODEFECERITOMNIS
NECGENUSUNDENOUAESTIRPISREUOCETURHABEBIT
TEMPUSETARCADIIMEMORANDAINUENTAMAGISTRI
PANDEREQUOQMODOCAESISIAMSAEPEIUUENCIS
INSINCERUSAPESTULERITCRUORALTIUSOMNEM
EXPEDIAMPRIMAREPETENSABORIGINEFAMAM
NAMQUAPELLAEIGENSFORTUNATACANOPI
ACCOLITEFFUSOSTAGNANTEMFLUMINENILUM
ETCIRCUMPICTISUEHITURSUARURAPHASELIS
QUAQPHARETRATAEUICINIAPERSIDISURGET

CODEX MEDICEUS: *Georgics* IV, 262–292

tur, "their fragmentary character precludes the possibility of securing an adequate basis for investigating the interrelationship of these manuscripts."

Let us now briefly examine them, one by one.

Codex Augusteus

Of this manuscript, dating possibly as early as the second or third century, there are only seven leaves extant: four in the Vatican Library and three in the Royal Library at Berlin.

The leaves in the Vatican once belonged to Claude Dupuy and came into the possession of the Vatican after the death of Fulvio Orsini (1600), to whom Dupuy had presented them. The Berlin leaves were bought at a sale at The Hague in 1862.

Schedae Vaticanae, No. 3225

This is one of the most celebrated of the existing manuscripts of Virgil and probably dates from the fourth century. It is in the Vatican Library. There are only seventy-five leaves, containing about a quarter of Virgil's works. It is notable for its illustrations of which there are fifty of different sizes, six of them being the full size of the page. The writing is in rustic capitals.

Sabbadini[5] reports that he has found in this manuscript evidence proving that it was produced in Spain, where it underwent correction by some scribe in the tenth century. It later came into the hands of the Italian statesman and author, Pontanus (1426–1503), afterwards belonged to Cardinal Bembo and then to Fulvio Orsini, from whose library it passed into the Vatican.

This manuscript was published by Bottari at Rome in 1741, with the illustrations (a copy of this book is in the Princeton University Library) and the manuscript itself has been more recently reproduced by photography (Plate II).

Codex Mediceus

In the Laurentian Library in Florence. It is written in capital letters of the fifth century. There are two hundred and twenty leaves, and it contains nearly the whole of the *Eclogues*, *Georgics*, and *Æneid*.

[5]R. Sabbadini, *P. Vergili Maronis Æneidos Libri I, II, III* (Turin, 1918), praefatio, vii, n. 3.

This manuscript was preserved in the Middle Ages in the Monastery of Bobbio and was still there as late as the middle of the fifteenth century. At the end of the sixteenth it belonged to Cardinal Antonio Del Monte and, afterwards, to Pope Julius III.

Subsequently it found its way to the Vatican but was afterwards returned to Cardinal Innocenzo Del Monte who refused to part with it. After his death in 1577, however, his heirs sold the book to the Medici who placed it in the Laurentian Library, where it has remained ever since, except, to use Chatelain's words, "for a short journey which it made to Paris from 1797 to 1815." This, being interpreted, means that in 1797 Napoleon stole the book and brought it to Paris and that it was returned by the Allies after Waterloo. While Napoleon had the book in Paris, it was bound in red morocco with the imperial eagles stamped in gold on its sides, and it was thus when I held it in my hands some twenty-five years ago. I have just learned that this binding has been removed.

This codex was published by Foggini in Florence in 1741, and now I hear that the Italian Government has decided to reproduce it by photography in commemoration of the anniversary that we are celebrating (Plate III).

Codex Romanus, No. 3867

In the Vatican Library. In capitals and ascribed by scholars to the sixth century. This manuscript has three hundred and nine leaves and contains all the three major works of Virgil, although there are a few lacunae.

The large illustrations, with which it is adorned, are much cruder than those of the Schedae Vaticanae No. 3225. There are nineteen of them in all and they were published by Bottari. The entire manuscript has since been reproduced by photography.

This manuscript was, at one time, in the Monastery of Saint Denys, near Paris, but since the fifteenth century it has been in the Vatican Library.

Sanguineis ebuli bacis: minioq; rubentem:
Et quis erit modus inquit? amor nó talia curat.
Nec lachrymis crudelis amor: nec gramina riuis
Nec cytiso: saturantur apes. nec fronde capellæ.
Tristis at ille tamen cantabitis Arcades inquit:
Montibus hæc uestris soli cantare periti
Arcades. o mihi tum: q̃ molliter ossa quiescent:
Vestra meos olim si fistula dicat amores.
Atq; utinam ex uobis unus: uestriq; fuissem
Aut custos gregis: aut maturæ uinitor uuæ.
Certe siue mihi Phyllis: siue esset Amyntas:
Seu quicunq; furor: quid tú: si fuscus Amyntas?
Et nigræ uiolæ sunt: & uaccinia nigra.
Mecum inter salices lenta sub uite iaceret.
Serta mihi legeret Phyllis. cantaret Amyntas.
Hic gelidi fontes. hic mollia prata Lycori.
Hic nemus. hic ipso tecum consumerer æuo.
Nunc insanus amor: duri me martis in armis:
Tela inter media: atq; aduersos detinet hostes.
Tu procul a patria: nec sit mihi credere tantum.
Alpinas ab dura niues: & frigora rheni
Me sine sola uides. ah te ne frigora lædant.
Ah tibi ne teneras glacies secet aspera plantas.
Ibo: & chalcidico quæ sunt mihi condita uersu
Carmina: pastoris Siculi meditabor auena.
Certum est in siluis: inter spelæa ferarum:
Malle pati. tenerisq; meos incidere amores
Arboribus. crescent illæ. crescetis amores.
Interea mixtis lustrabo Menala Nymphis.
Aut acres uenabor apros. non me ulla uetabūt
Frigora: Parthenios canibus circundare saltus.
Iam mihi per rupes uideor: lucosq; sonantes:
Ire: libet Partho torquere Cydonia cornu
Spicula: tanq̃ hæc sit nostri medicina furoris.
Aut deus ille: malis hominum: mitescere discat.
Iam neq; Amadryades rursus: nec carmina nobis
Ipsa placent. ipsæ rursus concedite siluæ.
Non illum nostri possunt mutare labores.

Nec si frigoribus mediis: Hebrumq; bibamus:
Scythomasq; niues hyemis subeamus aquosæ.
Nec si cum moriens alta liberaret in ulmo:
Aethiopum uersemus oues: sub sydere cancri.
Omnia uincit amor. & nos cedamus amori.
Hec sat erit diuæ: uestrum cecinisse poetam,
Dum sedet: & gracili fiscellam texit hibisco.
Pierides: uos hæc facietis maxima Gallo.
Gallo: cuius amor tantum mihi crescit in horas:
Quantum uere nouo: uiridis se subiicit alnus.
Surgamus. solet esse grauis cantantibus umbra.
Iuniperi grauis umbra. nocēt & frugibus umbræ.
Ite domum saturæ: uenit Hesperus: ite capellæ

QVid faciat lætas segetes: quæ sydera seruet
Agricola: ut facilē terram proscindat aratris:
Sæmina quo iacienda modo: cultusq; locorum:
Edocuit: messes magno olim fænore reddi.

QVid faciat lætas segetes:
quo sydere terram
Vertere mecenas: ulmisq;
adiungere uites.
Conueniat: quæ cura boum:
quis cultus: habendo
Sit pecori: atq; apibus
quanta experientia parcis:
Hinc canere incipiam. uos o clarissima mundi
Lumina: labentem cælo quæ ducitis annum:
Liber: & alma Ceres: uestro si numine tellus
Chaoniam pingui glandem mutauit arista.
Poculaq; inuentis Acheloia miscuit uuis.
Et uos agrestum præsentia numina Fauni
Ferte simul: Fauniq; pedem: Dryadesq; puellæ:
Munera uestra cano. tuq; o cui prima frementē
Fudit equum: magno tellus percussa tridenti:
Neptunne. & cultor nemorum: cui pinguia Cææ.

THE FIRST ROMAN EDITION: *Ecologues* X, 27–77; *Georgics* I, 1–14

Codex Palatinus, No. 1631

Also in the Vatican. The volume contains five hundred and seventy-one leaves, if one includes the sheets of white paper which the binder inserted between each pair of leaves. The manuscript is written in capitals, of the fourth or the fifth century. At one time it was in the Bibliotheca Palatina, at Heidelberg, but was taken to Rome in 1622. As in the case of the *Codex Mediceus*, it "took the trip" to Paris in 1797 and was returned to the Vatican in 1815. Thirty-three leaves have been lost.

Schedae Sangallenses

In the Library of the Chapter House at Saint Gall. In capitals and, according to Chatelain, possibly of the fourth century. Unfortunately, there are only eleven leaves of the text, containing some lines from the *Georgics* and some from the *Æneid*.

Schedae Veronenses

This famous manuscript contains three hundred and forty-four leaves, of which one hundred and twenty-eight are palimpsest; under a portion of a text of Saint Gregory's *Moralia in Job*, which is in Merovingian script, are discernible parts of the text of Virgil in capital letters and remains of Livy's First Decade in uncial letters. There are only fifty-one leaves belonging to a Virgil manuscript. Each page contains thirteen lines and the large margins are frequently filled with notes in cursive Roman script, perhaps of the same time as the text. These scholia were first published by Cardinal Mai in 1818.

Chatelain regards the Virgilian portion as dating possibly from the fourth century.

These seven manuscripts that we have described are all in capital letters, chiefly rustic in character. They were followed by a large number of minuscule manuscripts dating from the ninth century on. Possibly there are two to three hundred of these extant. Professor Schanz says, in the work quoted above: "Compared with these old witnesses, the more recent manuscripts can claim no especial authority." Nevertheless, we are fortunate to have here in Princeton, in the collection loaned by Mr. Robert Garrett, two leaves of one of them of the tenth century. For those who desire to go further into this subject, I refer to M. Schanz, *Geschichte der römischen Litteratur* (Munich 1911), II, 1, and to Chatelain, *Paléographie des Classiques Latins* (Paris 1884–1900), I.

Our review of the history of the text now brings us to the time of the invention of printing. In 1464, two printers, Germans by birth, who had worked with Fust in Mainz, by name Conrad Sweynheym and Arnold Pannartz, started out for Rome. On their way there, they stopped at Subiaco, where there was the Monastery of Saint Scholastica, and set up the first printing press in Italy. They remained in Subiaco about two years, and, in the autumn of 1467, moved to Rome. Once there, they put themselves under the patronage of the powerful family of the Massimi and, not later than 1469, they produced what is generally considered to be the first printed edition of Virgil (Plate IV). The book is undated but we know that it was not later than 1469, because in the dedication the editor states that Virgil was the first Latin poet printed by Sweynheym and Pannartz, and these printers published Lucan with the date 1469.

This edition of Virgil consisted of two hundred and seventy-five copies of which, unfortunately, only six or seven have survived. I am glad to say that one of these can be seen in the Treasure Room of Princeton University Library.

In the meanwhile, printing presses were starting up throughout Europe, and, owing to the great popularity of Virgil, his works were issued on all sides. It is difficult for us who are accustomed to the printed book to realize what the invention of printing meant to scholars and with what avidity printed books were sought after.

Taking our poet as an example, from the catalogues of libraries, either those that have been printed, or from manuscript catalogues that I have had made for my own use, I estimate that there were not far from one hundred and fifty different impressions of what may be called *Virgiliana* printed before 1501. I use the term "Virgiliana" in a somewhat restricted sense, meaning his works in whole or in part, in the original or in translation, but not including lives or commentaries. The Princeton University Library possesses a considerable

PLATE V

F eruidus :aſt illi ſoluuntur frigore membra
V itaq; cũ gemitu fugit indignata ſub umbras.

Progenitus ſpira formis monumenta maronis
Hęc uindelinus ſcripſit apud uenetos.
Laudent ergo alii polycletos parrhaſioſue
Et quoſuis alios id genus artifices.
Ingenuas quiſquis muſarum diligit artes
In primis ipſum laudibus afficiet.
Nec uero tantum quia multa uolumina: quantũ
Q; perpulchra ſimul optimaq; exhibeat.

.M.CCCC.LXX.

COLOPHON OF DI SPIRA'S EDITION OF 1470

Plate VI

Incipit liber primus æneidis fœliciter·

Arma, uirumq; cano: troiæ qui p̄mus. ab oris
Italiam fato profugus, lauinaq; uenit
Littora· multū ille, & t'ris iactatus, & alto:
Vi superū· sæuæ memorē iunonis ob iram·
Multa quoq; & bello passus: dum conderet urbem·
Inferetq; deos latio, genus unde latinum:
Albaniq; patres, atq; altæ mœnia romæ;
Musa mihi causas memora: quo numine læso:
Quid ue dolens regina deum: tot uoluere casus
Insignem pietate uirum: tot adire labores
Impulerit· tantæ ne animis cælestibus iræ:
Vrbs antiqua fuit (tyrii tenuere coloni)
Cartago· italiam contra, tyberinaq; longe
Ostia· diues opum, studiisq; asperrima belli·
Quam iuno fertur terris magis omnibus unam:
Posthabita coluisse samo· hic illius arma:
Hic currus fuit· hoc regnum dea gentibus esse:
(Si qua fata sinant) iam tum tenditq;, fouetq;·
Progeniem· sed enim troiano a sanguine duci
Audierat: tyrias olim quæ uerteret arces·
Hinc populum late regem, belloq; superbum:
Venturum excidio lybiæ· sic uoluere parcas·
Id metuens, ueterisq; memor saturnia belli:
Prima quod ad troiam pro caris gesserat argis·
Nec dum etiam causæ irarum: sæuiq; dolores
Exciderant animo· manet alta mente repostum
Iudicium paridis· spretæq; iniuria formæ·
Et genus inuisum: & rapti Ganymedis honores·
His accensa super: iactatos æquore toto
Troas, relliquias danaum, atq; immitis achilli:

The Sorbonne Virgil: *Æneid* I, 1–30

number of these early Virgils. In addition to the *Editio Princeps*, about which I have already spoken, there is to be seen in Princeton University Library a copy of the first edition with a date. This was printed by Vindelin di Spira, in Venice in 1470 (Plate V). Also worthy of mention are a beautiful edition of the *Eclogues* by Eggesteyn in Strasbourg, 1470, and a Virgil printed in Paris, at the Sorbonne, not later than 1472. This is the first Virgil printed in France and is the only complete copy known, the sole other exemplar, that in the Rylands Library in Manchester, containing only the *Eclogues* and *Georgics*. This copy, recently acquired from a wine merchant at Bordeaux, is in my opinion the most important addition to the Princeton Virgil collection that has been made in many years (Plate VI).

I believe you will find many other editions in the Library that will be of interest to you. I hope you will notice there a book which is rather poorly printed and not very attractive to look at. I refer to the Virgil printed at Brescia in 1473 (Plate VII). It is the first book printed there, and there is only one other copy known.

There are three books, moreover, to which I should particularly like to call your attention. It is true that they do not properly come within the scope of this paper, but they are germane to the subject and are of great interest and importance: namely, the *Commentary of Servius* on Virgil,[6] printed by the Cennini in Florence, 1471–72, and reputed to be the first book printed there; *le Livre des Eneides*,[7] printed by Guillaume le Roy at Lyons in 1483, a prose romance based on the *Æneid*, and the *Book of Eneydos*,[8] printed by Caxton in Westminster in 1490, an English translation of the preceding work—the first English "Virgil."

We now come to the end of the fifteenth century and we see the founding of the great publishing houses. Among these was the house of Aldus Manutius in Venice, to whom scholarship probably owes more than to any publishers who have ever lived, and who, as

[6] By the kindness of the Morgan Library in New York a copy of this book was loaned to the Exhibition of Virgiliana held in the Art Museum of Princeton University during the autumn of 1929.

[7] A copy of this book was generously loaned for exhibition by Dr. A. S. W. Rosenbach.

[8] Loaned for exhibition by the Morgan Library in New York.

Renouard[9] says, "sacrificed advantages of reputation and fortune and devoted their whole life to saving the ancient authors from the chaos into which eight centuries of barbarism had plunged them." The list of books published and carefully edited by Aldus is astonishing: almost a complete list of the writings of the great authors of antiquity, especially the Greek. His was the house which gave to the world the first editions of Æschylus, Aristophanes, Aristotle, Demosthenes, Euripides, Herodotus, Pindar, Plato, Sophocles, Strabo, and Thucydides.

He conceived the idea of making smaller books, more portable than the folios and quartos, and less expensive. He engaged Francis of Bologna to cut types based on the handwriting of Petrarch and, in 1501, began to publish a series of the great Greek, Latin, and Italian authors in duodecimo, using this new type which we now know as italic. The first book in the series was a Virgil (Plate VIII). The house of Aldus lasted about a hundred years and during that period published no less than twenty editions of our poet.

During this century several other publishing houses started up in Europe: Giunta in Florence and Venice; the Estiennes in Paris; Plantin in Antwerp—to mention probably the three most famous after Aldus. These houses all printed Virgils and, in each case, several editions.

In the seventeenth century, we have the Elzevirs at Leyden and Amsterdam, the last of whose editions, printed in 1676, had a great reputation owing to its having been edited by Nicolas Heinsius, who, Dibdin says,[10] "seems to have been born for the restoration of Roman poetry and who devoted thirty years to the emendation of Virgil's text, from collating a great number of ancient manuscripts." This century also saw the two editions, the *Variorium* and *Ad Usum Delphini*, the latter forming part of the series of classics published for the use of the Dauphin.

[9] A. A. Renouard, *Notice sur la vie et les ouvrages des trois Manuce* (Paris, 1803), Preface.
[10] T. F. Dibdin, *An Introduction to the Knowledge of Rare and Valuable Editions of the Greek and Latin Classics* (ed. 4, London, 1927), II. 549.

PLATE VII

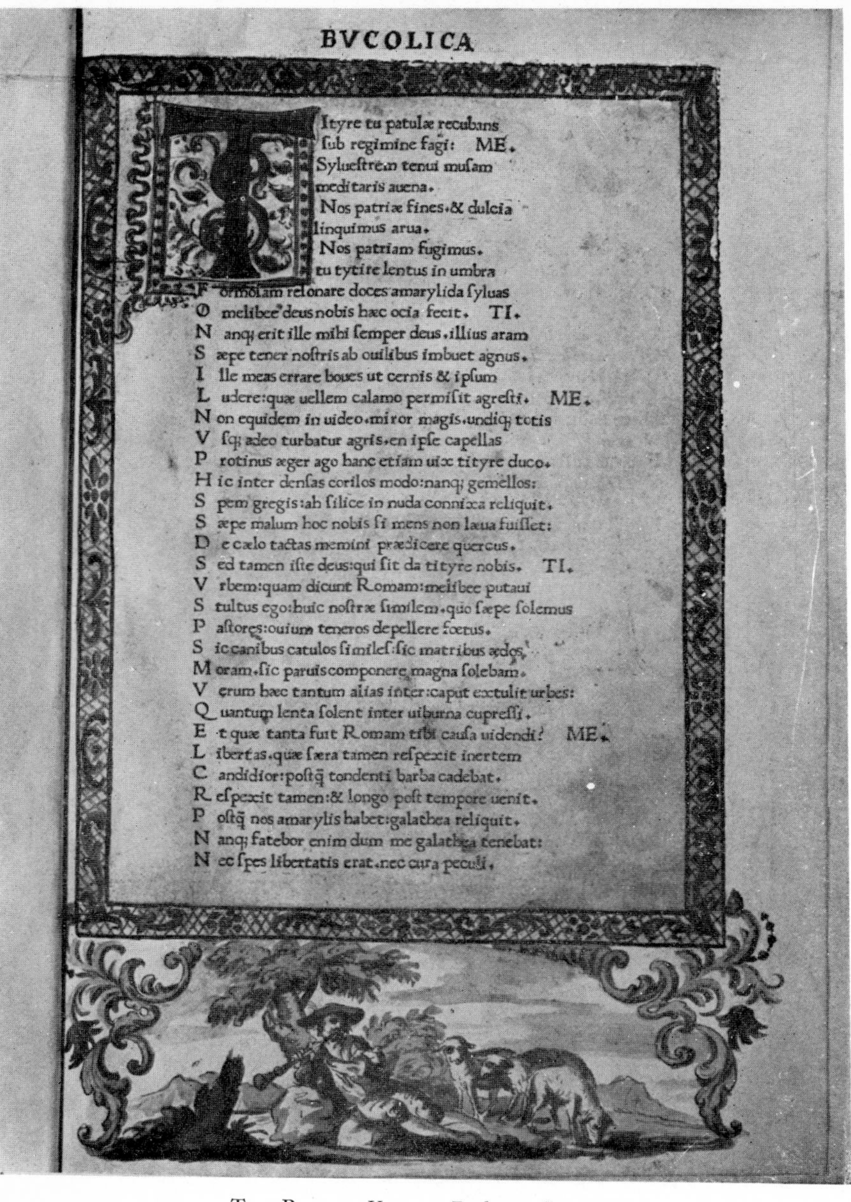

BVCOLICA

T Ityre tu patulæ recubans
ſub regimine fagi: ME.
Syluestrem tenui muſam
meditaris auena.
Nos patriæ fines. & dulcia
linquimus arua.
Nos patriam fugimus.
tu tytire lentus in umbra
Formoſam reſonare doces amarylida ſyluas
O melibee deus nobis hæc ocia fecit. TI.
N anq; erit ille mihi ſemper deus. illius aram
S æpe tener noſtris ab ouilibus imbuet agnus.
I lle meas errare boues ut cernis & ipſum
L udere: quæ uellem calamo permiſit agreſti. ME.
N on equidem inuideo. miror magis. undiq; totis
V ſq; adeo turbatur agris. en ipſe capellas
P rotinus æger ago hanc etiam uix tityre duco.
H ic inter denſas corilos modo: nanq; gemellos:
S pem gregis: ah ſilice in nuda connixa reliquit.
S æpe malum hoc nobis ſi mens non læua fuiſſet:
D e cælo tactas memini prædicere quercus.
S ed tamen iſte deus: qui ſit da tityre nobis. TI.
V rbem: quam dicunt Romam: melibee putaui
S tultus ego: huic noſtræ ſimilem. quo ſæpe ſolemus
P aſtores: ouium teneros depellere foetus.
S ic canibus catulos ſimiles: ſic matribus ædos
M oram. ſic paruis componere magna ſolebam.
V erum hæc tantum alias inter: caput extulit urbes:
Q uantum lenta ſolent inter uiburna cupreſſi.
E t quæ tanta fuit Romam tibi cauſa uidendi? ME.
L ibertas. quæ ſera tamen reſpexit inertem
C andidior: poſtq̃ tondenti barba cadebat.
R eſpexit tamen: & longo poſt tempore uenit.
P oſtq̃ nos amarylis habet: galathea reliquit.
N anq; fatebor enim dum me galathea tenebat:
N ec ſpes libertatis erat. nec cura peculi.

THE BRESCIA VIRGIL: *Ecologues* I, 1–32

PLATE VIII

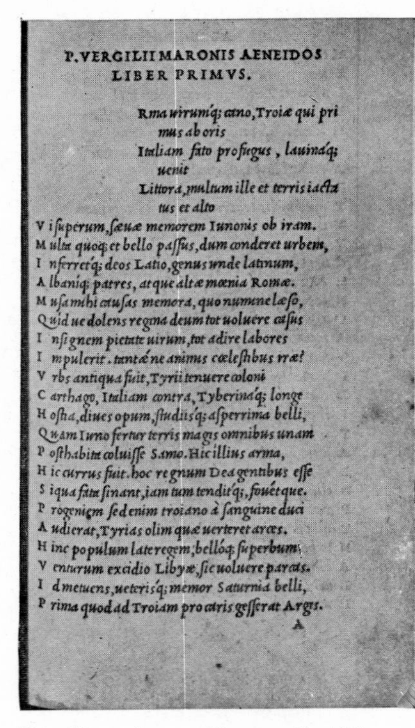
P. VERGILII MARONIS AENEIDOS
LIBER PRIMVS.

Rma uirumq́; cano, Troiæ qui pri
mus ab oris
Italiam fato profugus, lauinaq́;
uenit
Littora, multum ille et terris iacta
tus et alto
V i superum, sæuæ memorem Iunonis ob iram.
M ulta quoq; et bello passus, dum conderet urbem,
I nferretq́; deos Latio, genus unde latinum,
A lbaniq; patres, atque altæ mœnia Romæ.
M usa mihi causas memora, quo numine læso,
Q uid ue dolens regina deum tot uoluere casus
I nsignem pietate uirum, tot adire labores
I mpulerit. tantæ ne animis cœlestibus iræ?
V rbs antiqua fuit, Tyrii tenuere coloni
C arthago, Italiam contra, Tyberinaq́; longe
H ostia, diues opum, studiisq́; asperrima belli,
Q uam Iuno fertur terris magis omnibus unam
P osthabita coluisse Samo. Hic illius arma,
H ic currus fuit. hoc regnum Dea gentibus esse
S i qua fata sinant, iam tum tenditq́;, fouetque.
P rogeniem sed enim troiano à sanguine duci
A udierat, Tyrias olim quæ uerteret arces.
H inc populum late regem, belloq; superbum
V enturum excidio Libyæ, sic uoluere parcas.
I d metuens, ueterisq́; memor Saturnia belli,
P rima quod ad Troiam pro caris gesserat Argis.
A

THE FIRST ALDINE VIRGIL: *Æneid* I, 1–24

In the next century, the eighteenth, there were Jacob Tonson at Cambridge, John Baskerville at Birmingham, and Foulis at Glasgow, each of whom gave us handsomely and very correctly printed editions of Virgil. We must mention also the several editions produced by Heyne in Leipzig, 1767–1803, which Dibdin described[11] as "incomparable."

The last printer of this century that we will mention was Didot who published a Virgil in 1791. This house continued to publish editions of the poems until 1858. In the nineteenth century, among the editions of special importance are the Heyne-Wagner edition of Leipzig, 1830–41, and the editions of Conington, Ribbeck, Forbiger, and Benoist.

I have now attempted to give you a brief survey of the history of the text, from Virgil's autograph manuscripts to the present day and, I hope, I have shown you to what extent, since the invention of printing, his works have been published. For a book collector, and that is all I pretend to be, you can readily understand that a collection of editions of his work covers a large and interesting field. Everyone who had even a small library would be sure to have a Virgil and the large libraries many different editions. The dilettante, as well as the scholar, would have his copy. The result is that the collector can hope to find Virgils that have belonged to people of importance and interest. The publishers whom I have mentioned, as well as many others, vied with one another in publishing handsome editions, both as to typography and paper; many were printed on vellum. In each period, the services of the best artists have been called in to illustrate the books; the best binders, to bind copies. We thus have in a collection of Virgils an opportunity of gathering together books representative of every period in the history of printing, illustration, and binding, since printing was invented.

One may realize the truth of what I have said by examining the Virgils in the Treasure Room of Princeton University Library. In addition to the fifteenth century books, to which I have already referred, you will see several editions printed by Aldus and his fam-

[11] *op. cit.*, 559.

il y; besides the first, previously mentioned as printed in 1501, there is a copy of the third edition (1514), the only known copy printed on vellum; also of the edition of 1541, bound for the celebrated book collector, Grolier. The Grieninger edition of 1502, an interesting book with its curious woodcuts, should likewise be inspected, also various editions by the house of Giunta and by the Estiennes, the 1532 edition which belonged to Philip Melancthon, and shows his marginal notes. You will see the Plantin edition of 1575; the Elzevir editions of 1636 and 1676, the latter one of a few copies printed on large paper; the edition published in London by Ogilvy, 1658, remarkable for its engravings; the editions of Tonson, Baskerville, and Foulis, of which I have spoken; a copy of Didot's edition of 1791, printed on vellum and a copy of the same printer's 1798 edition, probably the most magnificent edition of Virgil ever published, with superb plates.

Junius S. Morgan

VIRGIL & DANTE

N THE opening verses of the *Divine Comedy*, that "medieval miracle of song" as Longfellow calls it, Dante tells us that he had lost his way in a dark and savage forest. It was April in the year 1300, and he was in his thirty-fifth year, half-way through the journey of life. How he had become lost he cannot explain, for he was overcome with sleep when he went astray from the right path. After wandering for a night, he finally sees a hill on which are shining the rays of the rising sun; but when he tries to reach the hill, his progress is impeded by a leopardess, a lion and a she-wolf, which drive him back toward the dark wood where the sun is silent. Suddenly there appears before him a man or the shade of a man, he is not sure which, and he calls for help. "I am not a man," is the reply, "but I was one, long ago; I was born under Caesar, and lived under Augustus, when men worshipped false and lying gods. A poet I was: I sang of the just son of Anchises who came from Troy when the proud city was burned. But why dost thou return to the distressful forest? Why dost thou not climb the mountain where there is joy?"

To this question Dante at first gives no answer; he is filled with wonder and awe—not at meeting the shade of a man who had long been dead, but at meeting the spirit of his best-loved poet; and he exclaims: "Art thou then that Virgil, that fount which pours forth so broad a stream of speech? O honor and light of other poets, count to my credit my long study, and the great love which has made me search thy writings! Thou art my master and my author, from whom I took the fair style that has brought me honor."

Then Virgil answers his own question: the hill must be attained not by the direct path, but by a longer and much more laborious route through Hell and Purgatory. So far Virgil can act as guide; but to lead Dante to Paradise there must be a guide who knew Christianity. And so the two poets set forth on their journey.

Obviously much in these introductory verses is symbolism—the dark forest of worldliness, the hill of righteousness, the sun of enlightenment, the three beasts, the shade of Virgil; and finally, Dante himself, a symbol of the human soul or of mankind in general. In considering the personages of the poem we must distinguish, however, between their symbolic value and their historic character; in particular, we must distinguish between Dante the protagonist of the action, whether taken literally or symbolically, and Dante the poet who writes of his fearsome journey after it is completed. Nevertheless, there is close connection between the protagonist and the poet, not merely because Dante tells his story in the first person and continually expresses his own sentiments and opinions, but because he relates in the form of poetic fiction his own spiritual experience. Early in life, apparently, he had determined to write a poem describing the afterworld from the Christian point of view, as Virgil in the sixth book of the *Æneid* had done from the pagan point of view; and this poem was to be a glorification of Beatrice, the woman in whose honor he had written his youthful lyrics. In his maturity, weighed down by the sad experience of exile, he returned to this project, with the purpose of pointing out the way of regeneration from the prevailing moral and political degradation of society. This purpose he carried out by showing his own spiritual development and progress. If the *Divine Comedy* were simply another example of medieval allegory, it would long ago have been forgotten; it lives today because it is a powerful piece of imaginative poetry which expresses in superb artistic form, and with fervid intensity and utter sincerity, the emotions of an individual human being.

Thus the symbols are not mere abstractions created out of nothing for the purpose of composing an allegory. Of course Dante accepted the medieval principle of the multiple interpretation of poetry: the obvious, literal meaning, whether fiction or history, is a veil which covers the true meaning. Thus the *Divine Comedy* is literally the narrative of his journey as a living man through the world of the dead, guided first by the shade of Virgil, and afterwards by his lady Beatrice who descends for the purpose from her seat in Heaven. Incidental to the main narrative are many episodic passages in which Dante in his own person pours out his eloquence on subjects of intense interest to him, ignoring for the time both fiction and symbolism. But the significance underlying the fictitious narrative is the escape of Everyman from the dark forest of sin and worldliness under the guidance of Reason. Our own enlightened human Reason is able to show us the true nature of sin and the means of avoiding it; but for the attainment of heavenly beatitude the human Reason alone, however enlightened it may be, is not sufficient, and the Revelation of divine truth is necessary. Virgil, then, stands for Reason in the highest development of which it is capable without a knowledge of Christian truth; and Beatrice stands for Revelation. Both are to Dante persons, just as he himself is a person; one of the arguments used to prove that Beatrice is a real person and not an abstraction, is the fact that Virgil in the *Divine Comedy*, as no one doubts, is the Roman poet whom Dante took as a model and whom he calls not only his leader and teacher, but his dear father. It is clear, then, that in forming his system of symbolism or allegory Dante did not personify the abstract qualities of Reason and Revelation, and give them names, but rather that he conceived of definite persons as representing two aspects of his own personality—the rational and the spiritual. Thus they stand in an intimate personal relation to him, and should be thought of not only as symbols but at the same time as individuals for whom he felt sincere and profound affection and admiration.

When properly understood, the two aspects of Virgil and of Beatrice, individual and symbolic, exist simultaneously and in perfect harmony. This becomes evident in the superbly described scene in Earthly Paradise, where Virgil is replaced by Beatrice as the guide. Virgil in his capacity as Reason has shown to Dante the sufferings of Hell and Purgatory, and can lead him no further; he does not immediately disappear from the picture, and angels quote from him the exquisite verse: "Manibus o date lilia plenis." Then Dante perceives the presence of Beatrice, as he feels once more the mysterious power of the love which had overcome him in his youth. Tremblingly he turns to speak to Virgil with the same trust with which a frightened child runs to its mother; but, he continues: "Virgil had now abandoned us, had left us without himself, Virgil my sweetest father, Virgil to whom for my salvation I had given myself." Even the delights of Eden cannot keep back his tears. These verses are addressed to no personified symbol; they express deep and sincere grief at the loss of a dearly loved friend, who must return to his abode in Limbo.

Dante's feeling of devotion to Virgil no doubt increased as he wrote the *Divine Comedy*, but it had begun long before. In the *New Life*, except for a casual reference to Homer whose works he could not read, Virgil is the first classic author that he quotes; and he tells us that he knew the *Æneid* by heart. Not only are many passages in the *Divine Comedy*, which it would take a long time to enumerate, influenced by the *Æneid*; Dante cites Virgil by name more frequently than any other writer, with one exception: Aristotle, the supreme scientific and philosophic authority, whom he calls "the master of those who know." Why then, we may ask, did he not choose Aristotle in preference to Virgil, as his symbol of Reason? Was the choice of Virgil purely arbitrary and personal? When he sought some historical character distinguished for wisdom, why did he pass over Cicero and Boethius, whose works, as he himself tells us, influenced him strongly? Did he consider Solomon or Cato, Saint Thomas Aquinas or Saint Bernard, to all of whom he gave positions of authority in the *Divine Comedy?* Could he not have chosen his fellow-townsman Brunetto Latini, who taught him, as he says, "how man makes himself eternal"? From our modern point of view, if strength of character or profundity of knowledge were Dante's criterion, he might well have chosen otherwise, and in fact he may have considered various possible choices. It is worth while, therefore, to inquire into the reasons which determined his final decision.

First of all, like Dante himself, Virgil was a poet, the greatest poet whom he knew, the example of perfection in poetic art. When Dante says in Canto I of the *Inferno* that from Virgil he derived his own poetic style, he naturally refers not to the imitation of specific passages but to the inspiration derived from study of an incomparably fine model; at that time he himself had composed impressive lyrical poems, but the *Divine Comedy* was still to come. It is also true, of course, that among the classical poets whom he knew, Dante found Virgil particularly suitable as a guide through the otherworld because in the *Æneid* the descent of Æneas to Hades is described. Although the arrangement of the lower regions is entirely different in the two poems, still Dante derived a number of features of his *Inferno*, and perhaps his main idea, from the description by Virgil; whereas he derived little or nothing from the numerous medieval visions of the hereafter. But even aside from this partial similarity of subject, Dante certainly believed that in the poetically created world of the *Divine Comedy* Virgil continued to act in accordance with his historical character, having simply learned in the spirit-world many things that were hidden from him during his life on earth. If to us Virgil is a supreme poet and nothing else than a poet, we must remember that in ancient times he was regarded also as one of the wisest of men, and that in both respects his fame had gone on increasing through the Middle Ages. His poems were used, like the Bible, in seeking counsel by letting the eye fall casually where the book chanced to open—the so-called Sortes Vergilianae. Numerous commentaries and biographies were composed, and even the common use of the *Æneid* in the study of grammar and rhetoric in the schools did not condemn it to oblivion. The noble ancients like Cato and Cicero and Virgil were revered in the Middle Ages as moral heroes, in anticipation of the critical appreciation of them that came with Humanism and the Renaissance. Moreover, just as the Greeks had done with Homer, so the pagan writers of the Roman Empire had interpreted the *Æneid* allegorically; and the Christian fathers, already familiar with allegorical interpretation of the Bible, adopted the same method with various Greek and Latin classics, and by so doing justified their interest in pagan literature. The *Æneid* in particular was so treated; it was believed to signify the successive periods in the life of man as he escapes from the slavery of error and vice, and reaches wisdom and virtue; so that Dante, who in his *Banquet* mentions this interpretation, might easily see an analogy between Virgil's poem and his own.

In the Middle Ages, partly as a result of the vigorous literary growth of his reputation, and partly through an extraordinary development of popular legends which clustered about his name, although some of them originally had had nothing to do with it, Virgil was traditionally believed to have had magical powers. Many of these legends grew up at Naples, where Virgil's tomb was a kind of shrine; and he came to be regarded as a protector, almost a patron saint, of the city. The universal reputation for wisdom which he enjoyed caused the attribution to him of a number of talismans which protected or benefited the city in various ways, such as the famous bronze fly which kept away all living flies, or the butcher's shop which kept meat fresh for months. But if these legends of Neapolitan origin became attached to Virgil on account of his literary fame and the known fact of his fondness for Naples, in the strictly literary and scholastic tradition his connection with Naples was of slight importance. It is not surprising, therefore, that miraculous deeds associated with other places were sometimes ascribed to him, such as the construction in Rome of a palace known as Salvatio Romae, in which were statues representing the various provinces of the empire; when any province meditated revolt, the corresponding statue gave the alarm by ringing a bell. This and similar legends were spread abroad by medieval travellers, only too ready, no doubt, to believe all the tales told to them by inhabitants of the Eternal City.

Now Dante gives no evidence that he believed any of the tales which made Virgil a magician or necromancer; some of them he must have heard, but he doubtless regarded them as puerilities unworthy of the great poet and sage. He did, however, accept one belief which was common to the learned clergy and the ignorant and superstitious masses alike. In the fourth *Eclogue*, Virgil uses Sibylline utterances to foretell the return of the golden age, the advent of a virgin (really the goddess of justice) and the birth of a child who was to rule the earth in peace and happiness. As early as the fourth century this passage was interpreted as a prophecy of the birth of Christ; and Virgil, though a pagan, was credited with having received divine inspiration. At a time when other ancient authors were frowned upon by the Christian church, Virgil was excepted from the general condemnation. But Dante, however much he may have desired to save the soul of Virgil from the consequences of living on earth at the time of paganism, does not make him a believer; rather he makes him a type of Reason which before the coming of Christ attained some of the ideals and principles of Christianity. This conception was necessary in the scheme of the *Divine Comedy*—his first guide being human Reason outside of Christianity yet in many respects in harmony with Christianity.

When Dante and Virgil have passed through the gate which bears the terrifying inscription "Abandon all hope, ye who enter," and have reached Limbo, the first circle of Hell, they are greeted by four other poets: Homer, Horace, Ovid and Lucan; to this group Virgil belongs, and he notes with approval that Dante is admitted as one of them. These famous poets of antiquity—not perhaps the five that modern critics would select as preeminent—and other sages and philosophers who lived blameless lives, are suspended in Limbo; their only punishment is to live in desire without hope, and Dante dwells long on the pathos of their situation. The counterpart to this scene occurs later, when the travellers have nearly reached the summit of the mountain of Purgatory. They are joined by a shade who makes himself known as Statius, the author of the *Thebaid* and the unfinished *Achilleid*, poems highly esteemed in imperial Rome and throughout the Middle Ages. In reality Statius doubtless lived and died a pagan, but Dante represents him as having been converted to Christianity by Virgil's fourth *Eclogue*, and led to repent of his sin of prodigality by a passage in the *Æneid* where the hunger for gold is condemned. In a quaintly humorous scene, Statius declares that in order to meet Virgil, to whom he owed not only (as is historically true) poetic inspiration, but also salvation, he would willingly delay his departure from Purgatory; and on learning that Virgil is actually before him, he bends to embrace his feet: "Per te poeta fui, per te cristiano." In beautiful and pathetic verses, he compares Virgil to a man walking in darkness who holds behind him a light to illuminate the path for others but not for himself. Allegorically, Statius represents Reason enlightened by Faith, an intermediary between Virgil —Reason deprived of Faith—on the one hand, and Beatrice—Revelation of divine truth—on the other hand. During the time that the three poets are together, Statius is allowed to explain to Dante several matters beyond the ken of Virgil; but after the appearance of Beatrice he remains silently in the background, and when Dante rises with Beatrice into the Heavenly Paradise, Statius presumably goes to his reward, but so far as the *Divine Comedy* is concerned, he is forgotten.

Not only was Virgil Dante's favorite poet, reputed to be a man of unrivalled wisdom, who had described Hades and had unknowingly prophesied the coming of Christ: another reason of equal importance with these impelled Dante to choose him as guide. The *Æneid* is the epic of Rome and Italy. It is not the spontaneous expression of the mind of a primitive people, but a literary epic, written with consummate art in an age of high culture, for the avowed purpose of showing forth the glory, power and magnificence of the Roman Empire. This fact, in addition to its artistic perfection and the wisdom contained in it, gave it supreme importance in Dante's eyes. The journey of Æneas to the underworld was justified because he had been chosen in Heaven as the father of Rome and of her empire, even though after his death he, like Virgil, was condemned for eternity to Limbo. In the *Æneid* Dante found abundant proof that Rome had been divinely ordained to rule the world, and he saw no reason to doubt that this mission was still in force. In the Middle Ages men were not conscious that the empire had come to an end, and that they were living in a period of transition between ancient and modern times. In theory, the Roman Empire was still supreme in civil affairs, just as the Roman Church was supreme in matters of religion. But the vitality of the imperial idea was diminishing; Italy was divided into independent and mutually antagonistic political units, while elsewhere in Europe the new nationalities were arising. Like most Italians of the day, Dante was at first patriotically devoted to his own city and only vaguely conscious of unity under the empire; but through his devotion to ancient Rome as interpreted to him by Virgil, he came to be one of the earliest and greatest representatives of Italian national feeling. He found for this feeling a solid basis in the abstract conception of a universal empire, which was to bring peace to all the world and her rightful position of honor to Italy. The fact that Christ had been born in a period of peace under the authority of Rome proved to him that the empire was a divine institution, like the church. In his poem the supreme sinners tormented by Lucifer himself in the lowest depth of the Inferno are Brutus and Cassius, betrayers of Caesar and therefore of the empire, along with Judas Iscariot, betrayer of the founder of Christianity.

Now the *Æneid* is the greatest poetic expression of the patriotism and the national feeling of ancient Rome; and its author was to Dante, not merely a poet, but, as he says, "our own greatest poet," "the glory of the Latin race" to which the Italians still belonged. Dante's strong national feeling was thus one of the chief reasons for his sympathy with Virgil. He believed that the ideal empire must necessarily be Italian, just as in ancient times the actual Roman empire had been Italian. But before this end could be attained for the honor and glory of Italy as a nation, it was necessary that all Italians should work together harmoniously, and that the Pope and the Emperor should refrain from infringing upon each other's duties and prerogatives. Since the authority of the Pope seemed more secure than that of the Emperor, and since the Papacy showed a tendency to interfere in political affairs, Dante appeared to incline in favor of the Empire; but in reality he strove to keep at equipoise the Cross and the imperial Eagle. His love of Italy was as strong as his love of truth. This is evident in the famous scene in Purgatory where Virgil and the troubadour Sordello embrace each other simply because they both came from one city, Mantua; Dante makes this scene the occasion of an eloquent condemnation of the Italians of his day, who by their partisanship and enmity and by their separatist policies kept Italy in turmoil so that her cities could not live at peace among themselves or even within their own walls, and the "garden of the Empire" had become a desert.

Thus whereas the fundamental idea of the *Divine Comedy* is the salvation of the human soul, in Dante's conception this was absolutely conditioned by political righteousness and this in turn by the dual system of world-government under Rome; so that the *Æneid* and the *Divine Comedy* have in common the practical aim of establishing and vindicating Roman authority. It matters not that Dante's scheme was impossible to carry out; the nobility of his purpose and the poetic genius which he showed in expounding and defending it have made him in modern times the great poet and prophet of united Italy; and in this aspect of his life and work, Virgil is his chief forerunner.

From this discussion it may be seen that in Dante's poem the two great moving forces—Reason and Religion—reach equilibrium and harmony, just as in his political theory the temporal and the spiritual authority should act in harmony. In accordance with the spirit of the age, it was natural for him to use personal symbols for these moving forces; and while at first sight the selection of Virgil may seem to need justification, the author of the *Æneid* as the symbol of Reason operating as an educative force through the medium of poetry is really the inevitable choice. The selection of Beatrice, the young woman whom Dante knew in Florence, as the other chief symbol is not so obvious on historic grounds; but it is sufficiently justified when we consider Dante's words concerning her at the beginning and the end of his youthful work, the *New Life*: By his love for her while she was on earth, his life was ruled and governed, but always with the faithful counsel of the Reason; and after her death he determined to write of her what had never been written of any woman. After all, his selection of companions for his journey to the otherworld could not be based on accidental or external considerations. These companions were not merely leaders and teachers; he identified them with himself through the choice of his heart and his life-long devotion to them as objects of his love, as is plain to every sympathetic reader of the *Divine Comedy*. And if the poem still stands without parallel in all literature as a memorial to a beloved woman, may we not say that it is also unparalleled as a monument erected by the affection of one great poet for another?

KENNETH McKENZIE

VIRGIL
AND THE ENGLISH MIND

E ARE met to wish Publius Vergilius Maro many happy returns of the day. Not that he is greatly in need of our encouragement. To be hale and hearty and still going strong at the mature age of two thousand, more or less, renders our wishes, however cordial, a bit superfluous.

But with Virgil and his fellow poets the hunger for fame was both a passion and a fashion; and as I have dwelt in mind upon this high feast and its meaning, I have liked to think that the good poet has not become so long and happily accustomed to his Elysian home among the "locos laetos et amoena virecta"—"the blessed seats among the lovely woods"—that he has forgotten this world of men which once deeply moved his great and tender heart, and cannot smile gratefully and approvingly upon this little attempt of ours to add to his towering monument of honor.

A birthday party is by no means a novelty for Virgil. Hardly was he two hundred years old when adoring poets were observing the feast with sacrifices, and heaping honors of a deified emperor upon his tomb. Virgil was a whole-souled ritualist, and no doubt revelled —with Elysian revelry—in that sort of program. But he had withal an eye for the sober facts, and if our manner of homage is less acceptable, as it is less ritualistic, yet it must be the more grateful, demonstrating as it does his fame and his prolific power still strong after two millenniums have gone.

For when all is said—and a good deal has been said in the course of these two thousand years—it is Virgil's peculiar distinction to stand preeminent as a towering mountain isthmus between the

Ancient and the Modern world. Other thoroughfares there are, but Virgil's is the high road, the beaten path, by which the subtlest and most precious influences have passed from the old civilization to the making of the new. As a poet he chose such themes as enabled him to gather an immense store of heroic legend, mythology, ritual, ideas, and tradition out of the dim past, already antique to him. He grows out of the old heroic poetry as a flourishing oak out of the stump of a primeval forest monarch. But with all these matters he mingles interests, and motives, and passions, which speak to the modern mind in its own idiom. His keen interest in physical science and natural causes is modern; his mastery of the grand passion and its subtleties is modern; his sense of the mystery and beauty of Nature and his love of lowly and homely life, his warm humanity, his eye for the picturesque, his sentimentality at times—all these are modern. Even his Alexandrian view and presentation of the ancient world as something antique and remote is like our modern way of regarding it. All these qualities tend to make Virgil, among the ancients, peculiarly intelligible to the modern reader, and recommend him unto our gentle senses. Perhaps then it is small wonder that in schools, through all the vicissitudes of fashions and variables of programs and curriculums and prescriptions for liberal education since ancient times, Virgil and his immortal poem have remained a constant, an indispensable, whether in the monastic schools, or the Grammar of the Trivium, or the schools of more humanistic times even to this moment. And the dog-eared copy of the *Æneid*, haled carelessly homeward in a bookstrap late in the day, by loitering boy or girl, is to me a reverend object and symbol of the ages.

What has been happening through countless long hours of nearly twenty centuries, in many a droning classroom? What is happening still, amid the "digging out," the perfunctory bad translation, the glossing, the gerund-grinding, the sing-song scansion, the comment? An altogether unpoetical business, one would say. And yet the glory of Virgil lies also in this, that, even when reduced to these lowest terms, his subtle influence and music are still alive, still passing into the fiber and being of the young and susceptible soul. Who can measure or guess his part in forming, refining, and sensitizing the susceptibilities of thousands of the undistinguished in every generation who have determined and still determine the character and texture of modern life? No other ancient poet, perhaps no modern poet even in our own language, is entitled to such a birthday honor.

While Virgil's formative influence has been lively among all European nations, his genius exhibits a strange affinity with that of far-off Britain—"toto divisos orbe Britannos."

The number of efforts to translate an author may indicate roughly the extent of his influence if not its quality. No foreign literary language more stubbornly resists a successful rendering in English than does Latin. And yet there have been more than twenty English versions of the major works of Virgil, besides twenty-five of the *Æneid* alone, and some one hundred and four versions of considerable portions of his entire works. Consider, too, the illustrious names among those whom Virgil's poetic quality has allured to this difficult undertaking—Douglas, Surrey, Waller, Dryden, Cowper, Wordsworth, Shelley, Morris.

Surely these mere matters of fact alone imply a deep affinity between the genius of Virgil and the Anglo-Saxon mind—far deeper than all vicissitudes of literary fashion. And I think that we may clearly discern certain marks of this poetic kinship.

First is the elegiac feeling common to both. For both Virgil and the English genius

> Sunt lacrimae rerum, et mentem mortalia tangunt.[1]

> Tears to human suffering are due;
> And mortal hopes defeated and o'erthrown
> Are mourned by man.[2]

From the Old English *Deor's Lament* and the *Wanderer* to Housman's *Last Poems*, lives the sense of pathos in life, especially the pity for both young and aged, helpless victims of life's overwhelming forces. Such also is Virgil's pity for Dido, Euryalus, Pallas, Lausus, for Evander and Latinus, yes, even for Turnus. Whether for these or for the athlete dying young, it is all one.

[1] *Aen.* I.462.
[2] Wordsworth, *Laodamia*.

Then in both Virgil and the Anglo-Saxon the religious and moral instincts are strong, and the patent and obvious signs of the poet's influence in our literature and life show a tendency to gather more closely in this region. That pervading sense common to both Æneas and his creator of an immanent deity, of a divine control of affairs towards one far-off purpose, that spirit and mind which sustains and pervades heaven and earth, manifest also in the primrose, and the light of setting suns and the round ocean and the living air, whether we meet it in Virgil, or Spenser, or Wordsworth, or Tennyson, is congenial and indigenous with us.

So too is Virgil's sense of moral values. For however concrete or phenomenal the matter with which he is dealing he seems to feel beneath it its moral and universal significance. Such a habit was no doubt encouraged by his passionate interest in philosophical studies, but it is deeper with him than training or schools. It is his genius. Hence his manner of expression is always tending towards grand generalization and gnomic utterance, but never beyond artistic bounds. This power, to be sure, is in part that of the genius of the Latin language, and Virgil shares it with other Latin poets, notably Horace. But in Horace it more often rises out of urbanity—is essentially transcendent *savoir faire*. In Virgil it springs from his poetic sense of fundamental beauty in commonalty spread. And in which of the Roman poets has it shown the variety and memorable beauty that it maintains in Virgil? Nor can one doubt that it was the abundance of this moral universality in him which tempted medieval men to find unintended moral allegory in the story of the *Æneid*, and to persist in so finding it for one thousand years, from fifth century Fulgentius through Bernard Silvester, John of Salisbury, Petrarch and Boccaccio, to the poet Spenser.

Virgil's moral affinity with the English mind is realized by the English poets themselves, not least by that most English of them, Ben Jonson:

> That which he hath writ
> Is with such judgment labor'd, and distilled
> Through all the needful uses of our lives,

That, could a man remember but his lines,
He should not touch at any serious point,
But he might breathe his spirit out of him.[3]

Ben Jonson is doubtless thinking especially of the little nuggets of moral wisdom, the proverbial phrases, the gnomic gems, which the poetic vein of Virgil so richly yields. Not to cite such worn and hackneyed bits as *hic labor, hoc opus*; *sic itur ad astra*, there are such as *degeneres animos timor arguit*; *scilicet omnibus est labor impendendus*; *monstrat amor verus patriae*; *res si qua diu mortalibus ulla est*; *summa dies et ineluctabile tempus*—precious fragments which have been collected out of his fabric and treasured up in hundreds. His phrases have for centuries been sounding in many an English ear, on many an English tongue. "Classical quotation," said Dr. Johnson, "is the parole of literary men all over the world." If he is right, Virgil of all the ancient poets is most responsible. At any rate, this power of grand poetic moral generalization is another point of strong sympathy between Virgil and the English genius—a genius, we may recall, which bred such poets as Shakespeare, Milton, Pope, Gray, Samuel Johnson, and Tennyson.

Not alone in his elegiac instinct, nor in his religious and moral strength, is Virgil a poet for the English. He is a passionate patriot; his heart is filled with the image of the essential Roman nature and the imperial Roman destiny. As he beheld the glories of the new empire unfolding under Augustus, he saw them as the natural, nay destined, fruit of that hard struggle with stubborn soil and weather out of which the Roman people had been wrought—without which they could not have been at all. Especially in the *Georgics*, but everywhere in his poetry, amid heroics or the Alexandrian artifice of the *Eclogues*, I catch the authentic smell of the soil in which he delighted, out of which he was bred, and from which his poetry grew as naturally as a forest elm. One of the most charming as well as significant episodes of the *Æneid* is Æneas' first sight of primitive Rome and his meeting with King Evander living in pastoral simplicity among his agrarian subjects.

[3] *Poetaster*, 5.1.

Facilisque oculos fert omnia circum
Æneas capiturque locis . . . . [4]

Æneas casts about his curious eyes,
New objects viewing still with new surprise,
With greedy joy inquires of various things,

—and Virgil too, one may be sure, in his mind's eye

passimque armenta videbat
Romanoque Foro . . . .

Saw cattle all about lowing in the Roman forum.

Empire out of agriculture—the Roman destiny. And the English destiny, too. The poet Spenser, friend of Raleigh and Leicester, was the first of English poets to dream the prophetic dream of British Empire. His great poem the *Faery Queen* is essentially the embodiment of this idea. The hero of his First Book, the Red Cross Knight, is none other than Saint George of England, bred incognito on a farm by farm-folk, as the best breeding Spenser could give him for his calling. Spenser, it would seem, was kin to Virgil in building his British Empire out of Georges—earthworkers—he had a strong smack for etymologies—and it is no unmeaning coincidence that the poet of the *Georgics* should find a hearkening ear in the nation that chose the peculiar protection of Saint George, and still cherishes the ideals of a landed aristocracy.

In the popular imagination of the later Middle Ages Virgil had grown to miraculous stature. He was remembered as a great magician or enchanter, and many were the legends of his wonder-working powers. Scholars incline to disparage this apotheosis of his memory. It seems to me significant. Was it a matter of mere historical accident that Virgil, not Horace, nor Ovid,[5] nor Homer—whose reputation was by hearsay very high—should be thus exalted and transfigured? I think not. I notice that critics at all times incline to speak not of the *influence* of Virgil, but of his *spell*—the *spell* which he casts upon the minds of others. To this enchantment the Anglo-Saxon

[4] *Aen.*, 8.310–11.
[5] Ovid too was something in this medieval way, but never even a competitor with Virgil.

mind, both youthful and mature, has been strongly susceptible and responsive, from its first contact with higher Roman culture.

But Virgil's glory is yet higher. He not only weaves his spell about the layman, but he is an enchanter of the poet's mind.

By his enchantment he has awakened, stimulated, trained, and heightened the native genius of English poets from the singer of *Beowulf* down. His part in the creation of English poetry cannot be measured. Speaking most superficially, he has bequeathed certain stock devices and motives of which poets never seem to tire, which never wear out—the mural decoration, the storm at sea, that woman so fair—or is she a goddess? she walks like one—the visit to the Lower World, the commerce with the dead, the voyage of life, the lady warrior. How these have charmed the poetic imagination through the ages! It is Virgil who establishes the enduring precedent of the epic sublimation of history—a precedent indispensable to Ariosto, Tasso, Ronsard, and Spenser, to mention only the most conspicuous.

Virgil is *par excellence* the poet's poet. Not all good and great poets are such. Some are great in themselves but sterilized. They produce few or no poetic offspring, no line of succession, no tradition. Virgil is perhaps the most prolific poet in this way who ever lived. For some thirteen centuries he has been not only bestowing devices and themes upon English poetry, but he has extended the poet's knowledge, he has refined and intensified our poetic phrase, attuned our poetic cadence, enlarged our poetic imagination, and taught the English poet the very architectonics of his work.

> Now the rich stream of music winds along,
> Deep, majestic, smooth and strong,
> Thro' verdant vales and Ceres' golden reign;
> Now rolling down the steep amain,
> Headlong, impetuous, see it pour;
> The rocks and nodding groves rebellow to the roar.

In this current Virgil is not only midstream, but he increases its volume and momentum, its power of nourishment and life to every shore it touches.

A moment ago I dared to include even the English *Beowulf* within the spell of Virgil. Scholars and critics have been too loth to accept what seems to me undeniable evidence of Virgilian schooling, in this and other Old English poems. They are held back, perhaps, by the romantic wish to admire in it only what is pagan and primitive and *Urenglisch.* They disparage the intrusion of Christian or Hellenic culture, and look askance at the evidence of classic refinement or suggestion.

But the fact remains that at least Virgil was read in the English monastic schools; he is quoted by Bede, was taught by Egbert at York, and imitated by Aldhelm and Alcuin. In the seventh and eighth centuries, the florescent period of Old English poetry, only out of the monastery came or could come the English poet. The miracle would be not the trace of Virgil in his work, but the absence of such traces.

In the *Æneid* these early English poets found, no doubt, elements of primitive heroic life which they could easily understand; but through these they found their way to what they needed far more—sophistication of style, thought, life, and art.

In Chaucer's time Virgil's subtly refining power is still at work. Externally the poetic enthusiasm for Virgil takes a different form, an emphasis of the romance of Dido under the auspices of the cult of courtly love. Dido becomes apotheosized as the faithful unhappy lady cruelly entreated, and Æneas the heartless traitor in love. Chaucer himself reviews the story of Books I to VI of the *Æneid* in some three hundred lines of the *Hous of Fame*, of which two hundred are devoted to the tragic tale of Dido; and he repeats the sad story with great power in some four hundred lines of his *Legend of Good Women.*

With the maturing Renaissance and the increasingly humanistic view of antiquity, one might expect the enchantment to weaken. If anything it has increased as it has become more intelligent. We may not here, even in summary, indicate what various English poets have severally owed to Virgil—Sidney, Spenser, Jonson and other dramatists, Dryden, Addison and his colleagues, Gray, Wordsworth—whether in phrase, device, idea, design, or music.

Parallel passages no doubt have their uses. Our annotations of English verse abound with them, especially with citations from Virgil, and no reader of English poetry thus edited needs be told how the glowing fragments of Virgil have mingled by thousands in the best modern poetical fabric, lending it life and fire and color, and ever enhancing in it the quality which is essentially poetical.

But parallel passages are only superficial evidence. Rather let a person well read in English poetry read and reread aloud certain passages of the *Æneid* and the *Georgics* and the *Eclogues*, and see whether they do not spontaneously awaken in him reminiscence of English poetical phrase or cadence or emotion, and stir in his mind's ear with sympathetic vibration the strings of many a modern lyre. It is for *him* to realize how deep and subtle and strong the life of Virgil as the poet's poet has continued to be for, lo, these two thousand years. Can you start the music of

> Plura domum tardis decedere plaustra juvencis,[6]

and not rouse that of

> The plowman homeward plods his weary way?

Poetic cadence, I realize, is a subtle and immeasurable matter. Who can declare the debt of English verse to the music of Virgil—or, for that matter, of English prose? Yet English verse and English prose as well must have wanted many a rhythm and many a resonance had the composer's ear not been early attuned to

> the stateliest measure ever moulded by the lips of man.

It was not in vain that Burke always had a ragged copy of Virgil "not far from his elbow," or that Johnson read through a book of Virgil each night and knew the *Eclogues* by heart, or that Tennyson's ear

> for half the day,
> The rich Virgilian rustic measure
> Of Lari Maxume, all the way
> Like ballad-burthen music kept.

[6] *Georg.*, 2.206.

Virgil's eye in fine frenzy is ever glancing from earth to heaven, and resting with peculiar tranquillity upon the nightly watchful spheres, the moon, the quiet night sky. At such moments a new and exalted tenderness comes into his voice:

> Sidera cuncta notat tacito labentia coelo.[7]
>
> He notes all
> The stars soft-gliding in the silent sky.
>
> Per amica silentia lunae.[8]

His eye lingers upon them, and dwells upon them with poetic and religious awe—

> Deum namque ire per omnia,
> Terrasque tractusque maris coelumque profundum.[9]
>
> For God his life
> To all the vast unbounded frame hath given,
> And runs through earth and air, and sea,
> and all the deep of heaven.

Now there may be two opinions whether Addison would have written the greatest lyric of his generation had he never known Virgil. I, for one, believe that it could not have been the greatest lyric had it not been informed by the peculiar Virgilian music and emotion of which I have been speaking.

> The spacious firmament on high,
> With all the blue ethereal sky
> And spangled heavens, a shining frame,
> Their great Original proclaim.
> Th' unwearied Sun from day to day,
> Does his Creator's power display;
> And publishes to every land
> The work of an Almighty hand.
>
> Soon as the evening shades prevail
> The Moon takes up the wondrous tale;
> And nightly to the listening Earth
> Repeats the story of her birth;

[7] *Aen.*, 3.515.
[8] *Aen.*, 2.255.
[9] *Georg.*, 4.222.

Whilst all the stars that round her burn,
And all the planets in their turn,
Confirm the tidings as they roll,
And spread the truth from pole to pole.

In Thomson's *Seasons* and in other important poetical premises of the Romantic Movement the *Georgics* play a determinant part. Says Burns, naturally enough: "the *Georgics* are to me by far the best of Virgil." Thus in schools and tendencies of the most divergent sort Virgil still has his proper part to play.

To that master workman in metrical mosaic, Tennyson, Virgil was indispensable. Many a tiny fragment he has picked up from the ancient poetical fabric which in itself seems inconsiderable or dull. But set with Tennyson's supreme skill into a piece of his careful design, it glows with unsuspected color, and both borrows and lends beauty in its new setting.

Or when through scudding drifts the rainy Hyades
Vext the dim sea.

This way and that dividing the swift mind.

To draw
The quiet night into her blood.

The moan of doves in immemorial elms.

The winds . . . Leaning upon the ridgèd sea.

Music that gentlier on the spirit lies,
Than tir'd eyelids upon tir'd eyes.

The Virgilian tradition has continued unbroken for two thousand years. Naturally it has passed through attenuated phases, but it has never ceased. Different poets in different ages have seen a different Virgil according to their variations; which is but another evidence of his power, and variety, and charm.

There remains, however, one higher measure of his poetic stature, and that is the necessity to their art which the greatest poets recognize in Virgil—particularly Dante and Milton.

One who bears in mind definite impressions of the personal quality of Milton and Virgil would probably be preoccupied with their differences rather than their kinship. Yet on a little reflection the points of sympathy that Milton doubtless felt with Virgil accumulate in surprising number—more than can here be told in detail.

They were alike in the very act of composition. It was Virgil's habit, at least in writing the *Georgics*, to dictate many lines early in the morning "under the first impulse of his inspiration, and to spend the rest of the day polishing and condensing them." So Milton could compose only "when the wakeful bird sings darkling" or "when morn purples the east." Says an anonymous contemporary: "He waking early . . . had commonly a good stock of verses ready against his amanuensis came." And Richardson: "He frequently composed lying in bed in a morning. . . . Then, at what hour soever, he rung for his daughter to secure what came. I have been also told he would dictate many, perhaps forty lines as it were in a breath, and then reduce them to half the number."

Virgil's soul, like Milton's, was "like a star and dwelt apart." And if Virgil seems the less austere of the two, he had less to make him so; though I suspect that on occasion he could serve stern notice on bores and intruders.

Both men were deeply religious, Virgil more inclined to ritual than at least the older Milton, though in Milton's heart there are signs of an idealized ritualism which for historical reasons does not emerge in practice.

Both poets are deeply and delicately sensitive to the heavens, the stars, and the night sky, "the mystical dance of starry spheres."

Both poets are moved by a strong national passion. Virgil believed in Rome. She was a nation chosen of God to awaken the world with her splendor—

> auspiciis illa incluta Roma
> Imperium terris, animos aequabit Olympo . . . .[10]

> Glorious Rome
> Shall bound her empire by the earth,
> Her pride by heaven.

[10] *Aen.*, 6.781.

Out of the world's chaos she would bring peace and order and one "aurea condet Saecula qui rursus Latio."

Similarly Milton believed in the English nation as a messianic example of liberty and enlightenment to the world. An eminent Virgilian scholar observes that the real subject of the *Æneid* is not "arma virumque," but the labor of founding Rome. A similar observation belongs to *Paradise Lost*, which is not the epic of Adam and Eve, nor of man's first disobedience, but an exemplar of the true personal liberty which is essential to political liberty, and is the hope of lasting English freedom and enlightenment.

Milton's intense patriotic hopes and despair which went to the making of *Paradise Lost* vibrate through the words, near the end, of the militant archangel:

> yet know withall,
> Since thy original lapse, true Libertie
> Is lost, which alwayes with right Reason dwells
> Twinn'd, and from her hath no dividual being:
> Reason in man obscur'd, or not obey'd,
> Immediately inordinate desires
> And upstart Passions catch the Government
> From Reason, and to servitude reduce
> Man till then free. Therefore since hee permits
> Within himself unworthie Powers to reign
> Over free Reason, God in Judgement just
> Subjects him from without to violent Lords;
> Who oft as undeservedly enthrall
> His outward freedom.

The kinship of mind and temper between Milton and Virgil is indeed close, but their kinship as poets and artists is even more apparent.

They were both born into times of Alexandrian culture and imbued with its best ideals. They both held that learning—not mere literary learning but encyclopedic learning—was essential to their art. They took all knowledge for their province—rhetoric, poetry, history, legend, science, philosophy, theology. Both submitted to life-long unsparing self-discipline in their art. Vast was the scope of their art and various their capacities, yet naught entered there of what validity and pitch so ever—whether their learning, their patriotism, their moral sense, their religious feeling, their joy in nature, their humanism, their passion for artistic perfection in style and structure—but that both had the peculiar genius which could fuse all these elements into one artistic whole. Not least of their acquisitive tastes was their common delight in old Greek and Roman myth. This rich hoard of old material they both regarded in the best Alexandrian manner, wistfully—as something antique, evanescent, transfigured in the sunset light of a Götterdämmerung. So that in their favorite use of it, it lends to the work of both something more intrinsic than superficial ornament or accessory. By it their work gains depth, texture, poetic intimation, the rich and complex splendor that is proper to the best Alexandrian work.

Both men were not only conscious artists but egoists. In this respect Milton seems to exceed Virgil; for in the face even of Aristotle and all epic precedent he falters not, but thrusts his own heroic soul forward into three at least of the finest passages of *Paradise Lost*; he thinly disguises himself in the tragic story of Samson, disturbs the season due of pastoral quiet in *Lycidas* with his high indignation, and in all his work is hardly hidden from view. The same characteristic of Virgil, if in smaller measure, appears in the *Georgics*, and perhaps more than we suspect in the other works. If one or other of two dear friends, Varius or Tucca, "whitest of souls" as Horace calls them, had had but a tincture of Boswell about them, how might their memoirs bring into high light the personal Virgil, veiled not only in the *Georgics*, but in the *Eclogues*, and even in the *Æneid*.

Two passages in our haste I venture to set side by side, not as parallels, for Milton is not a mere imitator of Virgil, aware as he may have been of the Virgilian precedent. These passages both intimate the deepest poetical and spiritual passions of the two, and I need not point out beyond citation the unison of tastes which they imply.

In the second of the *Georgics* Virgil sings:

> Me vero primum dulces ante omnia Musae,
> Quarum sacra fero ingenti percussus amore,
> Accipiant coelique vias et sidera monstrent. . . .[11]

[11] *Georg.*, 2.475 *ff.*

> Ye sacred Muses! with whose beauty fir'd,
> My soul is ravish'd, and my brain inspir'd—
> Whose priest I am, whose holy fillets wear—
> Would you your poet's first petition hear?
> Give me the ways of wand'ring stars to know,
> The depths of heav'n above, and earth below;
> Teach me the various labors of the moon,
> And whence proceed th'eclipses of the sun;
> Why flowing tides prevail upon the main,
> And in what dark recess they shrink again;
> What shakes the solid earth; what cause delays
> The summer nights, and shortens winter days.

Milton, still an eager undergraduate, but with accurate, if expansive, sense of his poetic future, thus addresses his native language:

> Yet I had rather if I were to chuse,
> Thy service in some graver subject use,
> Such as may make thee search thy coffers round,
> Before thou cloath my fancy in fit sound:
> Such where the deep transported mind may soare
> Above the wheeling poles, and at Heav'ns dore
> Look in, and see each blissful Deitie
> How he before the thunderous throne doth lie,
> Listening to what unshorn Apollo sings
> To th'touch of golden wires, while Hebe brings
> Immortal Nectar to her Kingly Sire:
> Then passing through the Spheres of watchful fire,
> And mistie Regions of wide air next under,
> And hills of Snow and lofts of piled Thunder,
> May tell at length how green-ey'd Neptune raves,
> In Heav'ns defiance mustering all his waves;
> Then sing of secret things that came to pass
> When Beldam Nature in her cradle was;
> And last of Kings and Queens and Hero's old,
> Such as the wise Demodocus once told
> In solemn Songs at King Alcinous feast,
> While sad Ulisses soul and all the rest
> Are held with his melodious harmonie
> In willing chains and sweet captivitie.

One might discern, if there were time, an analogy if not a parallel between the poetic biographies of Virgil and Milton. Rural and idyllic subjects engaged both in their earlier efforts, but with a difference. Virgil was farm-bred and more authentic in his poetic rusticity; Milton out of London touched the matter more exquisitely. Perhaps a comparison of Milton's *Comus* and his two idylls, *L'Allegro* and *Il Penseroso*, with certain of the minor works and the more mature *Georgics* should not be carried too far. But between *Lycidas*, the last of Milton's earlier poems, and Virgil's latest and ripest eclogue, the Tenth, the relation is more to the point.

Milton's earlier affinities in Latin verse, judging by his own metrical performance in that language, were closer to Ovid. But by the evidence Virgil was necessary to higher performance. That most exquisite, most musical, most poetical of all short poems in English could not have been what it is without Virgil. The Tenth Eclogue was necessary to *Lycidas*. The parallels between the two are obvious and have been oft rehearsed. But the kinship is deeper. Milton's poetic fervor has been heightened, the timbre and quality of his voice deepened, the delicacy of his feeling refined by admitting to his poetic soul the whole poetic power of his original. Dull would he be of ear who could not perceive how Milton has even transcended his great predecessor in such a passage as

> Where were ye Nymphs when the remorseless deep
> Clos'd o'er the head of your lov'd Lycidas?
> For neither were ye playing on the steep
> Where your old Bards, the famous Druids ly,
> Nor on the shaggy top of Mona high,
> Nor yet where Deva spreads her wisard stream.

Yet how impossible without

> Quae nemora aut qui vos saltus habuere, puellae
> Naiades, indigno cum Gallus amore peribat?
> Nam neque Parnasi vobis juga, nam neque Pindi
> Ulla moram fecere, neque Aonie Aganippe.

It is clear on reflection that the genius of Milton demanded a new and larger language to clothe his fancy in fit sound, and that he himself was creating this new medium. In *Lycidas*, and even here and there in his earlier poems, we catch prophetic intimations of the grander music and cadence of *Paradise Lost*, a new music in English, a music which included and indeed naturalized the deeper, fuller, more sustained diapasons of Virgil. To snatch but a fragment of the multitudinous store, I cannot but perceive a kinship—not a parallel—*that* is more obvious—between the tune of

> Ante tibi Eoae Atlantides abscondantur
> Gnosiaque ardentis decedat stella Coronae,[12]

and the tune of

> from Eastern Point
> Of Libra to the fleecie Starr that bears
> Andromeda far off Atlantick Seas
> Beyond th' Horizon.

Of vital importance was this new musical language to the greatest single poetic achievement in our language. Of vital importance also to lesser descendants—to Pope, Thomson, Cowper, Wordsworth. Milton, too, is a poet's poet, a receiver and enlarger of the poetic tradition.

The necessity of the *Æneid* to *Paradise Lost* is such that it appears in every consideration of the poem—of subject, mechanical detail, syntax, idiom, cadence, structure, temper, and final effect. Milton like Virgil, long choosing and beginning late, finds at length a subject of "prisca fides facto, sed fama perennis." His management of simile, spectacle, onomatopoeia, episode, rhetorical device, is Virgilian rather than Homeric, Alexandrian rather than primitive. This new medium of his, this new epic language must oft be construed as Virgilian Latin rather than English:

> Which when Beelzebub perceiv'd, then whom,
> Satan except, none higher sat, with grave
> Aspect he rose, and in his rising seem'd
> A Pillar of State; deep on his Front engraven
> Deliberation sat and publick care;
> And Princely counsel in his face yet shon,
> Majestick though in ruin: sage he stood
> With Atlantean shoulders fit to bear
> The weight of mightiest Monarchies; his look
> Drew audience and attention still as Night
> Or Summers Noon-tide air, while thus he spake.

[12] *Georg.*, I.221.

The kinship of Virgil and Milton asserts itself again in the fault which critics oftenest find with both. Neither, for all his fastidious choice, has been quite successful with his fable. Something is wrong in both, perhaps an archaeological remoteness from his story, which tends, in spite of the poet's best efforts, to an imperfect alliance between the tale and the process or art of telling it. Homer and the *Beowulf* poet were historically closer to the men and matter of their tales than Virgil to Æneas, or Milton to Adam and Eve, whatever he thought of their physical or spiritual parentage of mankind. Hence the necessary excess of supernatural interference in Virgil and in Milton, the inability of the hero's career to move under its own momentum, and the consequent glory and splendor of both poems, not in the tale's progress, but in episode—in the tragedy of Dido, or the remorse of Adam and Eve, the Council in Hell, or the funeral games, the first defection of Satan, or that of Turnus, or mere *tours de force* in simile, or grand symphonic elaborations on proper names. But what splendors these are—more varied and resourceful in Virgil perhaps, more heroic and exalted in Milton, but in either charged with the fullest vitality of which poetry is capable.

It is pleasant to indulge a fancy of the poet's return in person, on this his two thousandth birthday—tall, gaunt, grave, a little awkward and shy, surrounded, much to his discomfort, by interviewers, all clamoring to know what he has to say about present-day poetry. Not much probably. Perhaps in that soft, low voice of his we should hear only

sic omnia fatis
In peius ruere ac retro sublapsa referri . . . .

Thus all below, whether by Nature's curse
Or Fate's decree, degenerates still to worse.

However that may be, the fault is not his. Poet is he for ever; the less a poet is any singer who from his youth has not heard ringing in his ear the Virgilian song.

CHARLES GROSVENOR OSGOOD